WRITING IT DOWN

VICKI COBB
Pictures by Marylin Hafner

J. B. Lippincott   New York

Writing It Down
Text copyright © 1989 by Vicki Cobb
Illustrations copyright © 1989 by Marylin Hafner
Printed in the U.S.A. All rights reserved.
10 9 8 7 6 5 4 3 2 1
First Edition

Library of Congress Cataloging-in-Publication Data
Cobb, Vicki.
    Writing it down / by Vicki Cobb ; illustrated by Marylin Hafner — 1st ed.
        p.   cm.
    Summary: Simple descriptions of paper, pencils, pens, and crayons
explain how they work and how they were invented.
    ISBN 0-397-32326-3 : $. ISBN 0-397-32327-1 (lib. bdg.) : $
    1. Writing—Materials and instruments—Juvenile literature.
[1. Writing—Materials and instruments.]   I. Hafner, Marylin, ill.   II. Title.
Z45.C57 1989   88-14191
681'.6—dc19   CIP
                                                                      AC

Want to draw a picture? Want to write your name? The tools you need are all handy. Get some paper and a pencil or a pen or crayons. You are now ready to write.

Imagine what would happen if we suddenly didn't have writing tools.

Writing tools didn't always exist. Someone had to invent them.

PAPER

Paper is very flat and smooth, yet all paper is made of fuzz. Prove it yourself. Tear a sheet of paper and hold a torn edge up to the light. Look closely at the torn edge. Try different kinds of paper. Sure enough, there's always fuzz!

Scientists call the fuzz in paper *fibers.*

Paper is made with fibers and a secret ingredient: namely, water.

A Chinese man named Ts'ai Lun (*say lun*) thought up this great idea. Ts'ai Lun worked for a Chinese emperor about 1,800 years ago. Ts'ai Lun put bamboo and rags and fishnets in water. He beat them with clubs until they were fibers. Then he lifted out the fibers on a flat screen. The water drained away, leaving behind a flat, thin sheet.

Ts'ai Lun brought his new writing material to his emperor. No one had ever seen anything like it before. Ts'ai Lun's invention changed the world.

Before Ts'ai Lun invented paper, most people wrote on mats made of dried plant stems. These mats were called *papyrus* (*puh-PIE-rus*). Papyrus is very thick. Long pieces of papyrus were rolled up into scrolls. Papyrus was too thick to be piled in sheets, so there were no books.

Thin sheets of Ts'ai Lun's paper could be piled one on top of another. The sheets could be stuck together along one edge. That's how books came to be.

It's easy to open a book in the middle. Books replaced papyrus scrolls. Today the word *paper* comes from the word *papyrus.*

Paper was made by hand for more than 1,500 years.

1
CUT A 2-INCH SQUARE OF WIRE WINDOW SCREEN.

2
BEAT 20 SHEETS OF TOILET PAPER IN A QUART OF WATER.

3
ADD ½ CUP LIQUID LAUNDRY STARCH.

4
DIP THE SCREEN & LIFT IT OUT HORIZONTALLY SO THERE IS AN EVEN LAYER OF FIBERS ON IT.

5
PUT THE SCREEN & FIBERS BETWEEN LAYERS OF PAPER TOWELS & ROLL OUT THE WATER.

6
LET PAPER DRY ON THE SCREEN. WHEN DRY, PEEL IT OFF & WRITE ON IT.

Then, about two hundred years ago, a papermaking machine was invented. Instead of making paper sheet by sheet, the machine made huge rolls of paper.

When the machine was first invented, most paper fibers came from cloth rags. But now paper companies needed more fibers than they could get just from rags.

WHERE COULD THEY FIND TONS OF FIBERS?

TREES GO TO PAPER MILL →

WOODLAND 1

LUMBER CO.

CHIPS CHEMICALS

DIGESTER

HEAT, STEAM & CHEMICALS TURN CHIPS INTO MOIST FIBER BUNDLES

STEAM

5

6

BLOW TANK

PRESSURE CAUSES BUNDLES TO BURST APART INTO INDIVIDUAL FIBERS →

FIBERS GO INTO HEAD BOX

9

THE WATERY MIXTURE IS SPREAD IN AN EVEN MAT ACROSS AN

WIRE SECTION

WATER DRAINS OUT

ENDLESS BELT

PRESS SECTION

10

STEAM-FILLED DRYING SECTION

An inventor once got a great idea from a wasp nest. Wasps make paper nests from wood fibers. Their saliva dissolves the gluelike material holding wood fibers together. Today, paper pulp factories first chop up wood and then add chemicals to get out the fibers. Tons of fibers from the forests of the world become paper.

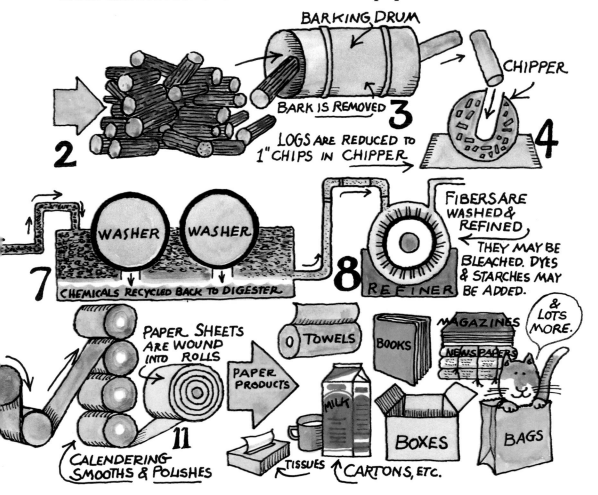

BARKING DRUM

BARK IS REMOVED **3**

LOGS ARE REDUCED TO 1" CHIPS IN CHIPPER

2

CHIPPER

4

WASHER WASHER

7 CHEMICALS RECYCLED BACK TO DIGESTER

8 REFINER

FIBERS ARE WASHED & REFINED, THEY MAY BE BLEACHED. DYES & STARCHES MAY BE ADDED.

& LOTS MORE.

PAPER SHEETS ARE WOUND INTO ROLLS

PAPER PRODUCTS

TOWELS BOOKS MAGAZINES NEWSPAPERS

MILK

11

CALENDERING SMOOTHS & POLISHES

TISSUES CARTONS, ETC. BOXES BAGS

BALLPOINT PENS

For thousands of years, the most important writing tool was pen and ink. But it was not an easy tool to use. A pen was made by carving a sharp point at the end of a goose feather.

Then the tip of the pen was dipped in ink. Every few words the pen had to be dipped again. It took a while for the fresh ink to dry, so a writer had to be careful not to smear his words.

Writing was a job for people who had special training. A professional writer was called a *scribe.*

Wouldn't it be a great idea to have a pen we didn't have to keep dipping in ink? That was the idea behind the fountain pen. A fountain pen has a little bag filled with ink that flows into the point. The fountain pen became much more popular than the feather pen. But the fountain pen wasn't perfect. It often leaked and made blotches, and fountain-pen ink also took time to dry.

The perfect pen wouldn't leak or make blotches. The ink would last a long time and dry quickly. It would be inexpensive.

About fifty years ago, two Hungarian brothers named Biro made the first ballpoint pens that worked well. They did not invent the idea of a ballpoint. The idea of a tiny ball that made its mark by rolling between ink and paper had been around for fifty years before the Biro brothers.

The Biro brothers discovered that they needed very thick, heavy ink to make the ballpoint work well, and they invented that ink. The heavy ink flows down toward the ball and coats it.

As the ball rolls, it keeps picking up new ink and rolling it onto the paper.

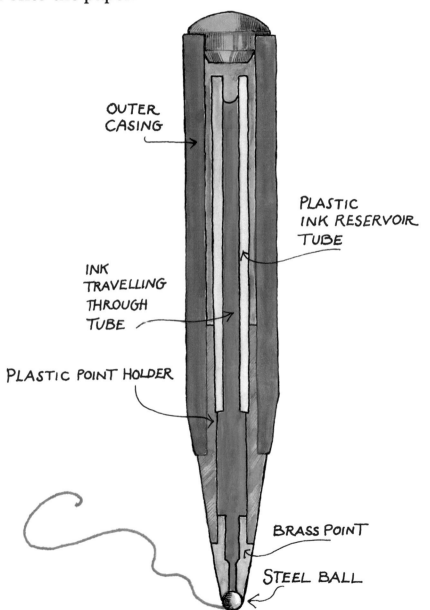

OUTER CASING

PLASTIC INK RESERVOIR TUBE

INK TRAVELLING THROUGH TUBE

PLASTIC POINT HOLDER

BRASS POINT

STEEL BALL

PENCILS

In the days when pen and ink were the main writing tools, people still needed a dry writing tool. Workers who measured land to make a road couldn't very well dip a pen while the wind was blowing. It was too messy. Some people used lead, a soft metal, as a dry writing tool. It made a very light mark.

People also knew about a very soft black stone that looked like a piece of coal, only it was much softer. When the stone was rubbed against another surface, it left behind a black mark that was much darker than the lead marks. The stone could be used for writing or drawing. We call this stone *graphite*.

Pure graphite is very dirty to use. Also, pure graphite is too soft to keep a point. When you write, you need a point to make a fine line.

How could graphite be turned into a useful writing tool?

About two hundred years ago, people mixed powdered graphite with fine clay and shaped it into thin sticks. After baking the sticks, they glued them between flat sticks of wood. The wood and graphite sandwich could be sharpened with a knife. It was a pencil! The graphite-and-clay stick is its lead. It is called *lead* because of the lead metal that at one time was used to write with.

Pencils are handy writing tools because they make a clear, dark line. But they are most useful because they let us make

The rubber eraser at the other end of a pencil will rub out graphite marks.

With a pencil as a writing tool

you can always change your mind.

THE CRAYON

If you want to draw a picture, it helps to have color. You can, of course, use paint. Paint has tiny pieces of colored bits called *pigment* spread through a liquid. You smear on the paint.

After the liquid dries, the pigment stays behind.

One of the first dry coloring tools was colored chalk. Chalk is soft, like graphite. It comes off when you rub it against paper. About one hundred years ago, schoolchildren used chalk to draw pictures.

The trouble with chalk is that it is very dusty. The teachers complained. That gave several inventors an idea. Why not put pigment into wax, instead of liquid?

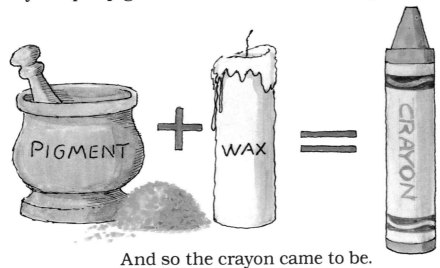

PIGMENT + WAX = CRAYON

And so the crayon came to be.

When you go to kindergarten, crayons are probably the very first writing tools you use. You can use them to make all kinds of designs.

Crayons are safe, dry, instant color. Use them to make bright, shiny, dust-free pictures.

Writing tools are used by people who create art and tell stories. You can be an artist or storyteller too.

EDUCATION